On Big Flowery Hill

On Big Flowery Hill

A soldier's journal of a secret mission into occupied China, 1942

John Hay

Preface by Jon Lee Anderson

Introduction by Peter Hay

Two Rivers Press
Reading

To the memory of John Hay
6 September 1916 – 4 November 1999

Edited and art directed by Peter Hay and Michelle Lizieri

Published in Great Britain in 2000 by

Two Rivers Press
35–39 London Street
Reading RG1 4PS

ISBN 1 901 677 09 5 (paperback)

ISBN 1 901 677 21 4 (hardback)

Printed by Riverside Printing Co. Ltd, Reading

To Pete

For persisting in completion of this project
despite lukewarm support from me

NOTE FROM THE EDITORS

The photographs in this book were taken on an Ensign-Selfix camera, Model '320' F/6.3, purchased in Burma. They are printed unretouched. The gashes, stains, and blotches in the images are marks of the journey – the films were developed en route in China and suffered from immersion in a paddy field. In structuring the book, while we tried to place photos in proximity to their corresponding diary entries, in some cases this has not been possible. All photos are captioned with dates and locations, enabling those readers who wish to do so to match images to text. We have edited the total number of diary entries down, but we have not altered the individual diary entries themselves. We have kept John Hay's spellings for place-names, which differ in some cases from conventional modern spellings but give similar results when pronounced.

May 1st. (Fri.) [LI-CHIA-PING]

Fatigues loading lorries on railway waggons.
Had Chinese meal in town in evening - very good.
Had long conversation with Mr Tong, speaks very good
English & is very Westernised. Some of Chinese Bn. left
by train tonight! Weather - wet.

May 2nd. (Sat.) [IN TRAIN]

Left store lorries in F.S.M.O. at 1200 hrs.
marched to station at Li-Chia-Ping. "Excellent"
accommodation in steel goods waggons. 1 waggon per
contingent!. Eventually made ourselves fairly comfortable
by removing boots and spreading out groundsheets &
blankets. Slept sardine fashion. Up stiff and uncomfortable.
Rations - bully and bread. Weather - wet.

May 3rd (Sun.) [IN TRAIN]

Train travelled very slowly with many stops.
Had a shower at water-tank last night. Stopped at a
station about 100 miles from Li-Chia-Ping at 0900 stayed
there till about 1200 then heard bad news that we are
returning to Li-Chia-Ping - move to Burma cancelled - no
reason apparent yet. News from Burma seems bad - Lashio
and Mandalay having fallen. Train returned towards
Li-Chia-Ping. Weather - fine.

May 4th (Mon) [LI-CHIA-PING]

Awakened in Li-Chia-Ping rly station.
Fatigues all day unloading our kit from waggons.
Back to same billet as yesterday afore. Many mosquito
here. Weather - fine & hot.

May 5th (Tue.) [LI-CHIA-PING]

Fatigues all day stacking stores. Helped Elliot
prepare evening meal. Got badly bitten on forehead
last night - bad time sleeping mosquitos. Rain

PREFACE

By Jon Lee Anderson

On the surface, this is the story of a disastrous journey that took place during the greatest human cataclysm of modern times, the Second World War. But there is much more to *On Big Flowery Hill* than that. As told through the photographs and personal journal entries of a young Englishman travelling through war-torn China, this is also the unfolding acount of a momentous, bittersweet interlude in the life of Johnny Hay. Through Hay, in turn, we become privy to the reality and to the perceptions of a different time – when there was still an Empire, when British soldiers ate Bully Beef and kept a stiff upper lip, and when they and the Chinese stared at each other across an incomprehensible divide. And finally, along with Hay, we are thrust back into the limbo of 1942, when an Allied victory was still far from certain, and war spread across the world.

Twenty-five-year-old Private Johnny Hay was languishing in an Egyptian desert transit camp with other soldiers from disbanded commando regiments when he signed up for the all-volunteer 204 British Military Mission to China. It was September 1941, and he had just been discharged from a hospital in Palestine after being treated for wounds suffered in Syria during a commando raid against German Nazi forces. Before long, Hay was in Burma, undergoing specialised jungle warfare training with other British and Australian volunteers. Their mission was to enter China, which Japan had already invaded, and to act as guerrilla warfare instructors and sabotage experts for the troops of Nationalist Chinese leader Chiang Kai Shek. Once Japan openly declared war, the men of the 204 Mission and their Nationalist Chinese allies were to carry out guerrilla raids to divert Japanese attentions from Allied forces elsewhere in Asia.

Hay and his comrades didn't have to wait long. In January 1942 – six weeks after the Japanese attack on Pearl Harbour – the 204 Mission's three battalions of fifty men each crossed into China on the Burma Road. As Hay recorded ebulliently just after crossing the frontier on January 23, they were received like heroes by Chinese troops at the roadside: 'We got plenty of cheering and waving'. His early photographs also reflect his own optimism: in one, a truckload of his fellow commandos, looking robust and healthy, smile and pose jauntily for his camera. In another, men in trucks overlook a gorge spanned by a suspension bridge. Challenges are being overcome, say the pictures, obstacles surmounted. After a week on the road, still reveling over his new adventure, Hay wrote excitedly: 'We must look like a lot of brigands with our filthy clothes and dusty faces!'

As things turned out, however, Hay and his friends had embarked on a 2,000-mile journey – by lorry, train, junk, sampan, and finally, on foot – to nowhere. Crippled by insufficient supplies and a critical lack of support from the Chinese forces they had been sent to help, the strength and morale of the men of the 204 Mission gradually succumbed to heat, hunger, malaria, dysentery and the crippling diarrhoea they sportingly called 'the skitters'.

Gradually, as the journey becomes an ordeal of survival, the early triumphalism of Hay's journal gives way to a grin-and-bear-it recording of the daily slog, accompanied by a reckoning of the distance covered, the state of the weather, and most importantly, what food he'd eaten that day. By July 2, the 204 Mission was travelling by foot, and things were bad. That evening, Hay wrote: 'Trouble with coolies deserting again… After midday started climbing very steep hills, then followed a stream downstream. Very tired and browned off at end of day, couldn't get fire to burn as no dry firewood. Had very little food today – 4 biscuits. Weather – very hot and sweaty all day. Distance 17 miles.'

By November 1942, only ten months after their arrival and reduced to only a handful of their original numbers, the 204 Military Mission to China was called off and disbanded, its remnants withdrawn from the field. Two months earlier, reduced to a mere shell of himself from the 'skitters', Private Johnny Hay had already been evacuated to Calcutta, India, where he was immediately hospitalized. After his first night there, his only comment about the place was: 'Grub very bad'.

For Johnny Hay, his Chinese wanderings were over, and no doubt he had few regrets about it at the time, but sixty years on, his journal and his photographs have survived to reveal that something of value also happened in his life on that journey. During the month of May, 1942, before things began to go truly downhill, Hay enjoyed an interlude on a mountain, Li Chia Ping, which he called 'Big Flowery Hill.' It was a fleeting idyll of sunny days spent on daily hikes to a grassy mountaintop where some of the men found a monastery with friendly monks. Their days were spent at a nearby pond where Hay and his friends swam and picnicked, read books and sunbathed. The days seemed long and glorious, and the war seemed far away. Johnny Hay took photographs of Chinese children, and in his journal, he tried to evoke in words the landscape he saw. One passage, written on May 10, 1942, feels timeless, somehow, as though it were written yesterday.

Below the frowning rock on which I sit the hill drops steeply down and divides into two spurs, silken green in the sunlight and hanging in folds like some exquisite and liquefying gown – so smooth are they that I feel as if I could reach out my hand and stroke them.

Clearly, different feelings of longing and desire imbued Johnny Hay's description of that landscape, but also a sense of awareness that at that very moment, he was living the greatest adventure of his life. On Big Flowery Hill, Hay's spirit soared, one feels, not only because of the beauty of what he saw, but at the realization of his own youth.

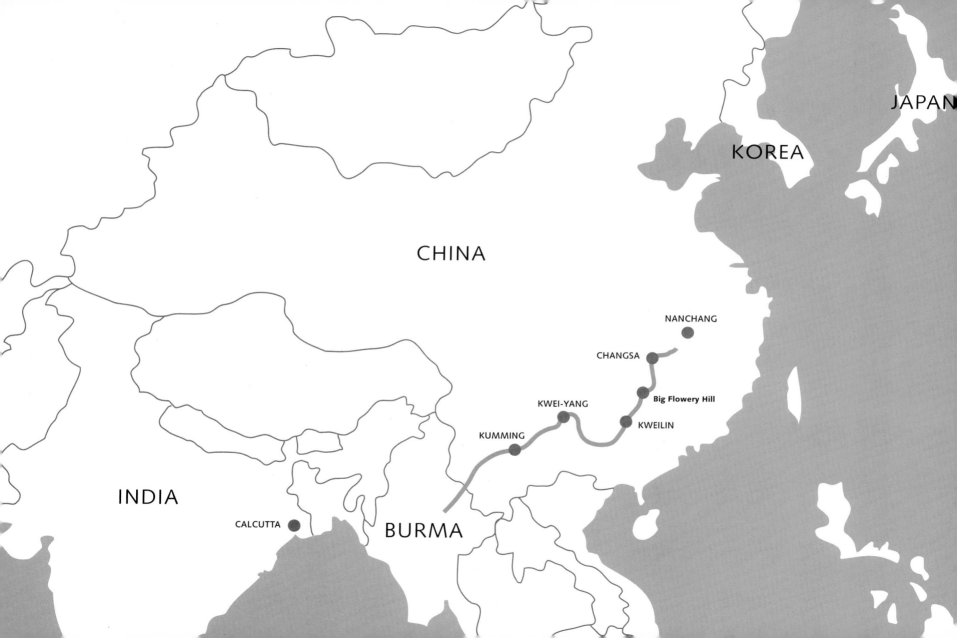

INTRODUCTION

by Peter Hay

Like the story told in my father's diary and photographs, the development of this book has followed its own meandering path. In 1979, my father loaned me some damaged negatives, photographs he had taken as a soldier in China in 1942. From them, he wanted me to print the images of Kweilin's limestone peaks, to match his memory to those ghosts of Sung Dynasty ink paintings. Concentrating on printing these selected portions of the classic Chinese landscape, I didn't check to see what other images were in the cardboard wallet. Then I lost track of the negatives for nearly twenty years. In 1996 the negatives surfaced mysteriously, tucked away in a tin medicine cabinet. My friend Gordon Carter, a photographer, made contact prints of the entire set. It was a revelation. I made a selection of the best images to print as a surprise present for Dad's 80th birthday.

Though my father did not talk much about his war experiences, everyone in the family knew about Dad and China after Mum brought home *The Forgotten Men*, by Iain Adamson, from the local library. That must have been sometime in the early sixties. The book told the story of the 204 British Military Mission to China. I remember the night Dad turned a page and saw his name: Private Johnny Hay. He was mentioned in passing as an example of British fortitude and stoicism. To us, the book's description of Dad's willful modesty seemed typical of him. Years later, in a bargain shop, I found several copies of *The Forgotten Men*, with the familiar rust-coloured cover and its drawing of trucks winding through a gorge. And years after that, in delayed synchronicity, Gordon's prints made from my father's old negatives included a nearly identical photo, one of trucks winding through a gorge.

When all the photos were printed, I saw they told a story. They were no longer just topography, distant mountains. That zig-zag of lightning against a hillside is the dust-white Burma Road. There are people: monks posing next to British soldiers; a wandering nomad with a drooping moustache, wearing a tattered patched coat; children gathering berries to stave off famine; children smiling. Shirtless soldiers sit sweltering in sunlight and shade inside a train while a uniformed official wafts a fan, perhaps to cool potential mutiny. Through the sequence of photos, the landscape changes as the diary does. Look at these images, and you embark on a journey that takes you across rugged ravined hills, over a waterfall, and across wide rivers, through the middle of nowhere, into mornings of clear cold dawn with miles still to travel.

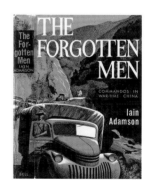

My father eventually showed me his diary, a battered brown notebook from Egypt, end-papered with a map of the Nile. From September 23rd, 1941 to December 27th, 1942, every day was scrupulously recorded in economically cramped script: miles travelled, weather, food. Especially food. And with the diary, Dad still had his curling contact prints, dated on the back. We matched diary entry to photo. I knew then that this was a book. In an unexpected sense, my father's wartime journey through China had finally found its destination.

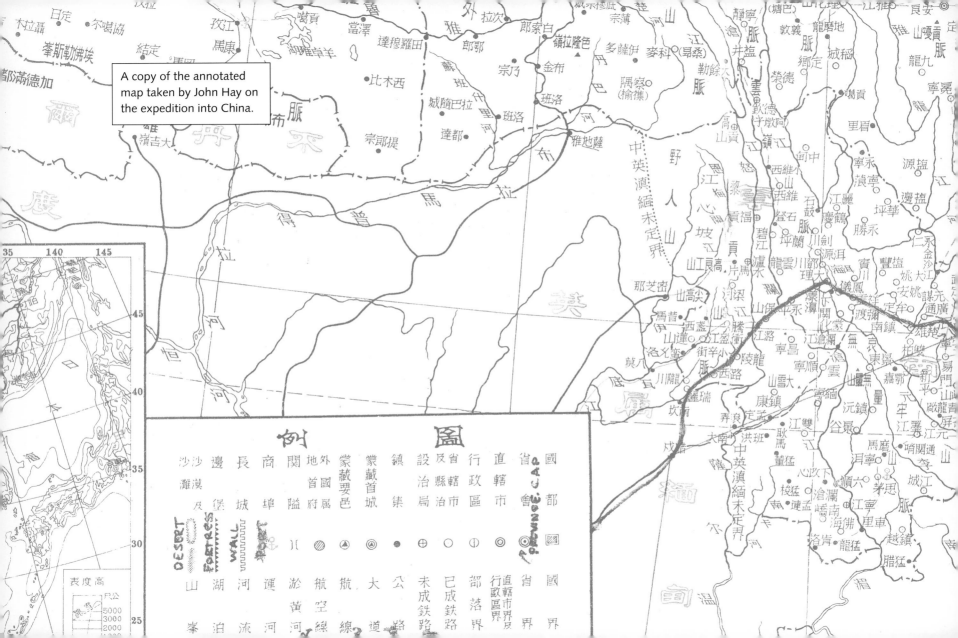

A copy of the annotated map taken by John Hay on the expedition into China.

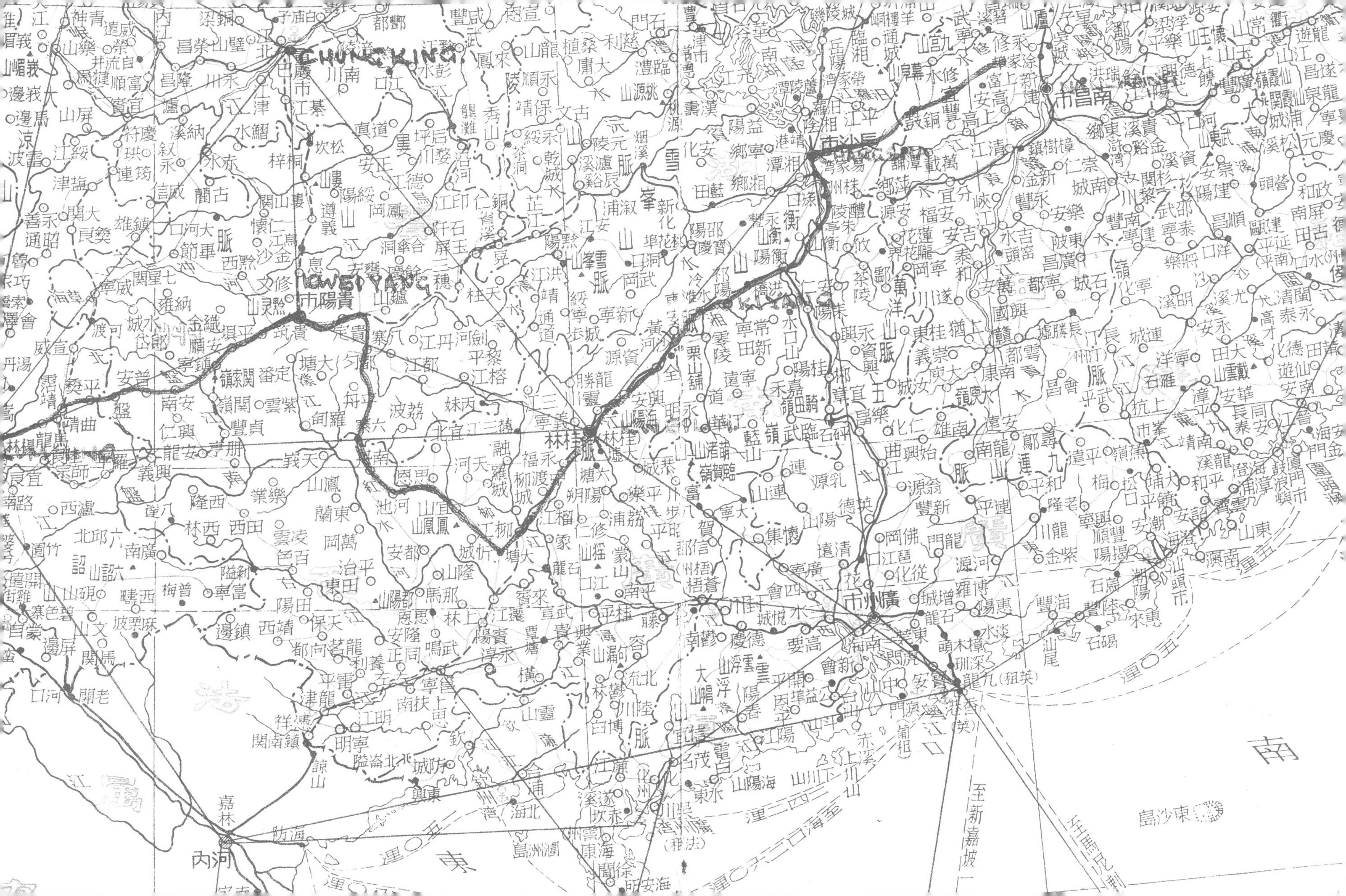
CHUNGKING
KWEIYANG

A Long Journey

Jan 22nd, Thursday [KYUKOK – BURMA ROAD]

Arrived here today at about 16.30 hrs. after the usual tiring
journey. Left Lashio at about 9.00 hrs., and had halt for bully beef
& bread at Kutkai. Very dull today and rather chilly all day. Plenty
of breathtaking scenery, hairpin bends, etc. Camping out tonight.
Have made bed down and put up mosquito net. Washed in river
which divides Burma & China. We are on Burma side of frontier.
Took photo' of huts, etc., on Burma Road. Bully and bread as usual
for supper. Chinese border town Wan-Ting. (112 miles today.)

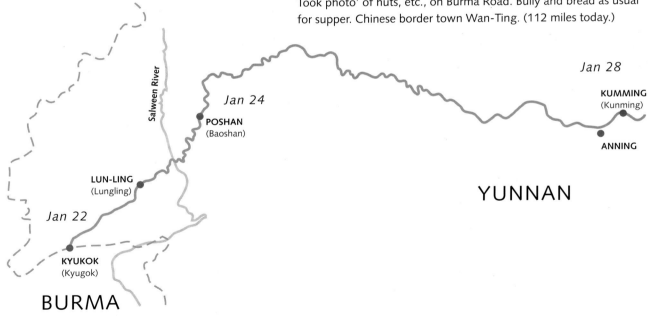

*Note to the reader:
See map of China
on previous page*

1 22.1.42   Kyukok – Waiting to cross into China from Burma

Jan 23rd, Friday [LUN-LING – CHINA]

Had a very good sleep last night – got up at about 6.00 hrs. this morning, moved off at 7.30 approx. Waited about at frontier – saw our first Chinese soldier. Took photo' of Kyukok from Chinese side. Very steep climb out of Kyukok, then descent into fertile valley – plenty of Chinese troops; all the way we got much cheering & waving. Had bully and biscuits for every meal as usual. Took photo' of mist in valley just after leaving border – it looked just like a valley of ice. Road was in pretty good condition most of the way, but in some parts it was very bad, and being repaired; huge gangs at work everywhere – they gave us plenty of cheers & thumbs up! Very steep climb with tortuous bends & sheer drops to Lun-Ling where we arrived at about 15.30; plenty of derelict trucks on & off the road, mostly down deep precipices. Took photo' at midday halt, also where we camped for the night here by the side of a shallow river. This is quite a large town but I don't suppose we'll be allowed out tonight. Made bed down & arranged mosquito net. Travelled about 85 miles today, and have been climbing most of the time.

Jan 24th, Saturday [POSHAN – BURMA ROAD]

Had a good sleep last night – very cold this morning, mosquito net was stiff with ice and my hat covered with white frost. Left Lun-Ling at about 7.30, very steep climb with the usual bends and very steep slopes. Took photo' of some glorious scenery near the Salween. Rose to altitude of over 9000 feet. Road very bumpy and dusty all the way. Crossed Salween River by suspension bridge – no Jap bombers today – took photo' of the bridge. Halted for lunch over other side of valley. Everybody a bit browned off as road very bumpy. Arrived here just as it was dark – bivouaced in field outside town – made up bed in dark near campfire; usual meals of bully and biscuits. Shaved by firelight. A bit of singing by the fireside tonight. Haven't seen town by daylight but seems pretty large and is walled. Have just refilled camera and sorted out kit for morning. Travelled about 106 miles today.

Jan 25th, Sunday [YUNG-PING – BURMA ROAD]

Awakened early this morning, very cold and mosquito net frosted in as usual. Travelled along bumpy & dusty road mostly on the level, road ran alongside Mekong for several miles. Crossed the river by suspension bridge – two suspension bridges in operation – one-way traffic; also a raft bridge and remains of a bridge presumably destroyed by bombing. Climbed for a couple of hours after leaving the river, carburettor trouble again – but soon righted. As usual gangs of stone-breakers all along roadside, dressed in the universal blue, a very large percentage of them have goitres in advanced state. Saw numerous derelict trucks on and off the road. Bully & biscuits as usual for breakfast & dinner. Arrived here about 18.00 hrs. Talked to well dressed Chinaman who is in charge of Bank of China here – told us today's news from the wireless – apparently we have captured a number of German generals and 15,000 prisoners in Libya – first news since we left Maymo. Got billets in a guest-house here – had a shave in hot water followed by Chinese meal of rice, meat, fish, cabbage, long shiny things like worms and many unrecognisable substances, all eaten with chopsticks. The Chinese seem very pleasant and pleased to see us, they are really very clean and cheerful. We have really seen so much of this grand scenery since we left Lashio though truck travelling is so tiring that we are beginning to take it all as a matter of course. Most of the time the road clings perilously against steep hillsides, which are terraced for rice even when the slope is as great as 6/1. The most striking scenery today was the Mekong river cut deep down in a sharp valley, blue as the Mediterranean against the shores of Cyprus, and as tortuous as the road itself. Very hot in sun today, but very cold this afternoon in the shade. Travelled about 85 miles today.

3 24.1.42 Waiting to cross the Salween

Jan 27th, Tuesday [NEAR ANNING]

Start delayed by one vehicle with a puncture. Geen's truck which was delayed yesterday morning by water in the petrol arrived during the night. A long journey today – we intended to do 180 kilos but actually did 216. Road pretty level and very dusty all the way. No halt for tea at midday on account of long journey. Passed several aeroplanes concealed in houses today, also Chinese parachutists and pilots – later on passed an aerodrome. Halted at dusk, camped by roadside; had a good meal tonight – bully stew mixed with tomato soup, peas, beans, followed by tinned peaches, biscuits and butter from our luxury box. Had a very painful shave in cold water. Extremely cold tonight. About 135 miles.

Jan 28th, Wednesday [KUMMING]

Awoke early this morning after a very cold and uncomfortable night – frost on my pillow. Tea and bully for breakfast. Else's truck which broke down 3 days ago arrived last night so that we now have our full convoy. Started off at about 8.30, comparatively flat country, bumpy & dusty roads. Very cold as usual so started off wearing scarf, gloves, greatcoat and balaclava – we must look like a lot of brigands with our filthy clothes and dusty faces! Passed a couple of factories in a valley – pretty recent construction. Roads much better condition today – still very dusty.

Everything went OK until midday halt when CO's truck had water filled in with petrol – delay to remedy same, then we got a large stone wedged between rear tyres – considerable labour to remove same by means of pulling with a strap and banging with a hatchet; CO's truck 'passed out' again – I bet he was fuming.

Next delay occurred when Geen ran his truck off the road and down the banking in a cloud of dust; I got myself & clothes thoroughly filthy fixing chains to our truck to pull him out! Regaining convoy about 10 miles from Kumming – everybody a bit annoyed with all the delays.

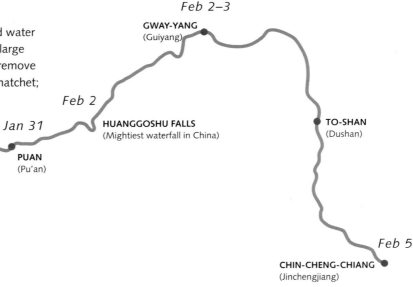

Feb 2–3

GWAY-YANG
(Guiyang)

Feb 2

Jan 31

HUANGGOSHU FALLS
(Mightiest waterfall in China)

TO-SHAN
(Dushan)

Jan 30

PUAN
(Pu'an)

CHAN-YI
(Zhanyi)

Feb 5

KUMMING
(Kunming)

CHIN-CHENG-CHIANG
(Jinchengjiang)

Jan 28–29

5 23.1.42 Campsite at Lun-Ling – Chinese troops crossing bridge

Arrived here 18.30 approx. & after a bit of messing around, eventually settled down in Rest-House here. Had a very much needed shower & changed my clothes, then an excellent Chinese meal – vegetable soup (I had two bowls full), rice, and ham omelette which I ate ravenously. We are settled down comfortably in billet with beds and a brazier going. Probably get a chance to look at the town tomorrow, anyway should have a comfortable sleep tonight. Travelled for about 50 miles alongside the track of what I presume is the new Lashio-Kumming railway – embankments, cuttings and tunnels are prepared but very little track laid. About 90 miles today.

6 27.1.42 Near Anning, Burma Road

7 27.1.42 Near Yunnan-Szi

Jan 30th, Friday [CHAN-YI]

Had good breakfast – 3 fried eggs, bread, jam, etc. Loaded trucks and sundry fatigues. Had talk from Consul wishing us best of luck, etc., left hostel at 12.00 approx. One or two halts on the way as CO's truck wasn't functioning too well. Flat road most of the way so made pretty good time. Distance travelled was about 110 miles. A very welcome surprise awaited us here – this place appears to be some sort of hostel, and it took some time to convince myself that one of the clean-sheeted beds in a room for 3 was for me. Had a good wash & shave in hot water – then followed dinner in a clean dining hall – soup, pork chops, roast potatoes, beans, and sweet served by immaculate English-speaking stewards. Last but not least the W.C. accommodation here is up to western standards – it is a long time since last I pulled a chain! Must get to bed now and try out this comfortable-looking bed. Just found out that this is an airport.

Jan 31st, Saturday [PUAN]

An excellent sleep last night, awakened about 7.30 – had good wash in warm water – breakfast was wonderful eggs, potatoes etc. followed by pancake. Usual hold-up (just after leaving Chan-yi) with trouble from C.O.'s truck. Good road all day – fairly flat for most of the journey. In the afternoon we started climbing thro' very rocky country with sugar-loaf hills. Crossed from Yunnan Province to Kwei-Chow Province today. Had 'chow' at Chinese rest-house at lunchtime – usual soup, egg dish & rice – quite good altho' not many of the boys enjoyed it. Excellent scenery this afternoon and this evening when we passed thro' very hilly country with many hair-pin bends. The hilltops silhouetted against the yellowing sunset looked like a graph of the rise & fall of our temperatures as we turned the hair-pins & passed vehicles on the bends. Took photo of village where we lunched, and of hilltops. 125 miles today.

Camped just outside Puan on paddy field – very bumpy; no water so have not washed or shaved yet. Am writing this by moonlight – full moon tonight.

Feb 1st, Sunday [60 MILES FROM PUAN]

Started off on time today, but had many delays during the day. One of the trucks hit another truck on an S-bend and damaged the radiator. Very hilly country all day today; one section of about a mile had about 30 hairpins – took photo' of same. Took photo' of some hilltops silhouetted against the sky like cardboard show cards. Camped again in paddy field on steep slope, my bed is on the edge of a precipice with about 40 ft. drop – think I'll have my feet that end! Writing this by moonlight again. Very much hotter during the day, and quite warm tonight. About 60 miles today.

9   28.1.42   Cadre Coy 204 BMM outside village near Kumming

Feb 2nd, Monday [GWAY-YANG]

Started off on time this morning at about 8.00 hrs. after a good warm sleep. Fairly hilly for first few hours with very sharp mountaintops, then rest of day travelled on pretty level downhill road through country clustered with pimply hilltops, steep cone-shaped rocks rising to 200 or 300 ft. About 90 miles from here crossed river on arch bridge of several spans, then a steep climb again, saw a wonderful waterfall (reputed to be 2nd highest in the world) took photo' of same which can never recapture the foaming white of the water falling and the oily blue of the pool below; also took photo' of bridge nearby (about 85 miles from Gway-Yang). Mostly downhill after this, thro' more pimply country. Arrived here at Gway-Choo Province at about 16.30. Billeted in barracks at hospital. Chinese 'chow' tonight. 126 miles today.

Feb 5th, Thursday [CHIEN-CHING-CHIANG]

Moved off on time 7.30 this morning after hasty wash and breakfast. This is our last day of truck-travelling, tonight we get a train to Hen-Yang. Very damp and misty again today, roads very slippery. Passed thro' same sort of country roads as we have seen for last 400 miles with hundreds of conical hills, coal seams evident on the surface in many places, railway cuttings etc. in course of construction. Has 'chow' at midday in small town with usual crowd of onlookers – food not very good today. Arrived at Chien-Ching-Chang at about 17.30, loaded three personal trucks on train, unloaded all stores into wagon. Am writing this in the train which has a very distinct sway, we started off a few minutes ago at 23.00 hrs. in 2nd class compartment, rather cramped.

About 125 miles today.

10 28.1.42 Village near Kumming. Fort guarding entrance

11 1.2.42 Hilltops near Puan (overleaf)

Feb 7th, Saturday [KI-YANG]

Rudely awakened at about 21.30 last night at Gway-Lin, got up from a comfortable bed to go and have an excellent supper & about 6 cups of good coffee and innumerable cakes. Apparently a slap-up meal had been prepared for us earlier in the evening but had been cancelled owing to our lateness. There were only a few of our squad there to appreciate the meal – but we took all the remnants with us for the boys to enjoy in the morning. Back to bed in our sleeper again – but it was some time before I got to sleep again, owing perhaps to the wakening effect of 6 cups of coffee! But more likely on account of the shunting of the train which continued for about an hour to the continual accompaniment of whistle blasts. Awakened at about 7.00 hrs. this morning feeling very warm and comfortable. Breakfast consisted of eggs and rice – supplemented this with peanuts and local rice-bread biscuits, etc. Had a shave, did a bit of reading and ate peanuts. Very cold and miserable, dull weather with rain again, train moving very slowly with many stops and starts. Arrived at station about 15 miles from here in dark and cold drizzling rain at about 17.30, crowded into our three trucks with all our own kit – then began the most fantastic journey I have ever made.

LI-CHIA-PING
(BIG FLOWERY HILL)
(Lijiaping)

Feb 7–April 26

KI-YANG
(Qiyang)

GWAY-LIN
(KWEILIN)
(Guilin)

KWANGSI

CHIN-CHENG-CHIANG
(Jinchengjiang)

Feb 5

Our first 12 miles or so was over fairly good roads thro' hilly country with the usual paddy fields, our headlights made a huge rainbow-like arc on the wet black sky before us, then we came to a village with narrow cobbled street. A Chinese officer led the way and we proceeded slowly with no more than a couple of inches clearance from the buildings on either side, our headlights picking out the eaves and balconies of the timber building and making grotesque slow-moving shadows across the street; incredulous and curious faces framed in crooked doorways looked up at us as we passed by the varied shops of this little community. We came to a sharp right-angle bend and it seemed as if we could never get the truck round – but we did so, scraping the corner-post of a shop, much to the distress of its occupant; passed thro' a length of roofed street with the top of the truck scraping the beams, then across a narrow river bridge and out into the country again thro' bent trees and paddy fields. Once again we traversed a village much the same as the first – then out again into the inky night thro' what seemed like an orange grove. An abrupt halt at the edge of the paddy fields with our headlights shining over expanses of differently levelled water separated by narrow dykes – across this morass in the wet blackness we carried our kit in three journeys to our billets here. Words cannot adequately describe the mystery and fantasy of this last lap of our 2000-mile journey. On arrival here we had a most unexpectedly good English cooked meal – soup, roast chicken and jam tart. Our billets are in an old ancestral home, we have an upper room for 9 of us with straw to sleep on, and warmed by the usual charcoal fires – all very comfortable and beyond our wildest hopes.

13 1.2.42   Between Puan and Gwan-Ang in Gwan Chow Province

14 30.1.42   Pin-An village between Kumming and Gwan-Ang

Feb 8th, Sunday [KI-YANG]

Had a very good sleep last night, reveille at 7.15 this morning, breakfast at 8 consisting of rice porridge, three fried eggs, tea and bread and butter (the butter has the consistency of our butter but tastes and smells rather like dripping). After breakfast, fatigues all morning carrying kit across from the trucks and storing demolitions in house some distance across the paddy fields – coolies carrying most amazing loads. Lunch of well-cooked meat, potatoes, carrots and spinach followed by lovely pancakes. Fatigues again this afternoon, then another dinner, roast beef, three vegetables and Swiss roll. Spent the evening organising my kit – rather distressed to find that I have lost 1 $^1/_2$ lb. of my cherished tobacco! Am writing this by rather inefficient candlelight. Had a little leaflet from officer commanding Chinese Surprising Battalions here – welcoming us here. Am agreeably surprised by conditions here which are very comfortable – the Chinese are very pleasant and amiable. We are situated in hilly country & surrounded by paddy fields.

Feb 9th, Monday [KI-YANG]

Very cold again today, drizzling with rain most of the time. Fatigues in morning unloading remaining kit. Stayed in during afternoon and had a very good hot bath in a large wooden tub. Meals are still keeping well up to the high standard at which they started. Did a bit of reading in the evening and met Mr Yu, our squad interpreter.

15 2.2.42   Near Gway-Yang

16 2.2.42   Near Gway-Yang

Feb 10th, Tuesday [KI-YANG]

Usual good sleep last night and a good shave in hot water this morning. Scrambled eggs for breakfast, curried meat rice and pancakes for dinner, and roast duck for tea – all of which I consumed in maximum quantity – this cold weather is making me very hungry. Fatigues in morning camouflaging truck. Played a game of chess. Went to nearby town Ki-Yang in afternoon, amazed to find that it is so large and possesses a number of substantial buildings. The town is alongside a very wide river which we cross via a slender & many-arched bridge. Shops are generally together in kind, i.e. there is a street of furniture shops, a street of printers, etc, and everywhere to be seen tobacconists, where the inmates sit rolling and cutting cigarettes. As at Kumming, the people are very curious & if ever we stopped to look in a shop we soon gathered an immense crowd – but everyone is polite & there seems to be no attempt to overcharge or swindle us. Bought a quilt (uncovered) for $26, but couldn't get a covered one as that entailed another trade. Stayed around our charcoal fire in the evening and taught Wally Marshall to play chess. Good soup again for supper tonight. Had lecture from CO who explained that we are now Coys *[Ed: Companys]* and would start training the Chinese in demolition work next week; we are to salute Chinese officers. It looks as if it will be a month or so before we commence operations.

Feb 11th, Wednesday [KI-YANG]

Very surprised this morning upon leaving my warm bed (quilt very warm) to find a layer of snow upon the ground; we certainly have experienced some changes in weather during the last few weeks. Good meals as usual today. Malay contingent arrived this evening. We had to turn out in the rain and help them unload their kit – they were all very surly & miserable as compared with us when we arrived with nobody to help us.

Feb 12th, Thursday [KI-YANG]

Snowed during the night again (still very cold this morning). First fatigue of day was getting one of 'Malaya's' trucks out of a paddy field. I spent $1^1/_2$ hrs. fixing skid chains to another truck which was to pull it out. After getting filthy dirty and cold beyond all feeling – finished fixing chains just as the damaged truck was set on the road again. Further truck-removing fatigues in afternoon. Started reading 'Poet's Pub' by Linklater – very amusing satire.

Feb 13th, Friday [KI-YANG]

'Route March' this morning – consisted of a march to town and a stroll around the town. Got paid today $70 at rate of exchange $75 to £1, which is most distressing! Spent evening reading – started 'High Table' by Joanna Cannan.

Feb 14th, Saturday [KI-YANG]

Started training our Chinese Battalion in demolitions today. CO gave lecture in English which was then translated into Chinese – a very slow and difficult process, especially as there are no Chinese equivalents for such terms as 'gelignite', ammonal, etc., however the Chinese seemed delighted by practical demonstrations. Very cold again today – but sun shone for a few minutes! – still snow on the ground. Lazy afternoon reading and gossiping. Chinese New Year festivities commence today.

Feb 15th, Sunday [KI-YANG]

No parades all day – spent day reading and playing chess. A bit of sunshine today. Chinese crackers going off all day.

Feb 16th, Monday [KI-YANG]

Commenced training Chinese Battalion in demolitions. Lecture from CO translated into Chinese by Mr Lancaster, who has excellent command of the language – very cold & boring for us. Played basketball in the afternoon. Played chess and did some reading in evening.

Feb 17th, Tuesday [KI-YANG]

More demolitions lectures today. Played basketball in morning. Heard that Singapore has fallen – find it difficult to understand. Usual evening diversions. Australians arrived tonight.

Feb 18th, Wednesday [KI-YANG]

Spent morning preparing explosives, etc., for Major Robinson's lecture tomorrow. Had a bath this afternoon. Had letter from Ralph via Chapman. Wrote to Ralph this afternoon for posting tomorrow.

Feb 19th, Thursday [KI-YANG]

Demolitions again today – Nobel's 808, did bore-hole charges in timber, cutting charges on steel rails etc., tried to cut $^3/_4$" sq N.S. rod with 2 x $^1/_4$ lb. scissors charge – unsuccessful – but OK with 1 lb. charge.

Feb 20th, Friday [KI-YANG]

Demolitions this morning. 'Goodwill' party this afternoon at Assembly Hall – whole school was present and we were seated 8 men to a table – 4 of us and 4 Chinese – our names were written in Chinese on a card on the table. Hall decorated with slogans such as 'Sino-British unity means victory for the democracies'. Had speech from General Le-Hu-An, return speech from Colonel Johnson via interpreters. 'Chow' was very good and I managed two bowls of rice in the best style, and spat my bones & gristle onto the floor with gusto. There was a Chinese Colonel, Major and Sergeant at our table; the Colonel spoke a little English and presented his card. After the chow which lasted nearly two hours we had a concert, commencing with the Chinese and our National Anthems played by Chinese Military band, which was quite good and struggled manfully thro' our anthem, not rushing it as most easterners are apt to. Concert started with singing by Chinese choir (Travelling Art & Drama Unit) with 6 sopranos and about 12 males – very good trained singing. Then followed Chinese boxing which is a display of contortionism by one man chasing himself around, then a play, very well-acted but rather difficult to understand, as it was mostly dialogue. Each of our contingents gave a show – singing, boxing, etc. Then followed another Chinese play, and we wound up with the 'fire ball' – a man swinging two pieces of charcoal on end of a wire. Quite a good friendly evening.

Feb 21st, Saturday [KI-YANG]

Demolitions this morning – missiles, sticky-tank bomb, grenades etc. Lecture in afternoon by Chinese general on Jap tactics – very long-winded and was never finished, as the interpreter seemed to have lost his notes, so General filled up time by discussing the last Jap attack on Changsha. Spent evening writing up Chinese notes and reading – started reading 'Surgeon's Log' – very good.

Feb 22nd, Sunday [KI-YANG]

Lazy day today, reading and dreaming. Had church service in dining hall today – by American missionary – excellent sermon, in fact best I have heard since being in the army. Usual evening.

Feb 23rd, Monday [KI-YANG]

Very warm day today – brilliant sunshine. Rifle inspection, game of basketball. Situation re Australia and Rangoon serious. Started wearing K.D. [Ed: Khaki Drill].

Feb 24th, Tuesday [KI-YANG]

Demolitions all day – very warm and pleasant. Thunderstorm at night. Was on 'hospital' duty all night guarding Watson who is still a bit 'puddled' – he thinks he is a Major & is still at Maymyo. Had a walk across country in the afternoon – at one place whole village turned out to gaze at us.

Feb 25th, Wednesday [KI-YANG]

Route march in morning – went up some colossal hills, finally climbing about 500 feet on a wet slippery slope of about 2 in 1. Very misty at top so didn't get a very good view. Came back to camp under our own steam and own route. Basketball in afternoon.

Feb 26th, Thursday [KI-YANG]

Went out to pagoda – on appreciation of situation – very fine day – warm sunshine. Hell of a row on because Robby found Stocky & Scott at top of pagoda which was supposed to be in enemy hands. Stocky got returned to duty and we all got promised parades on Sunday. Demolitions in afternoon – rock-blasting – by Major Dixon. Saw a Chinese tactical exercise, 'enemy' wore arm-bands with Jap badge, and were ambushed in a pass – 'Chinese' had live ammo' with brens & rifles, also live mortars – 'enemy' only had blanks! Those pretending to be shot did it so well that I thought they were really dead – I shouldn't be surprised if some were wounded.

Feb 27th, Friday [KI-YANG]

Spent first part of morning writing operational orders on yesterday's scheme, then had a very good game of basketball. Lecture on 'Mandarin' in afternoon. 'Robby' says my operation orders 'best he has ever seen'. Heard good news that we have sunk transports with about 80,000 Japs off Bali. Situation at Rangoon however seems very serious – if Rangoon falls we are rats in a trap! Spent evening helping Mr Gwok to learn English. Dergel beat me at chess!

Feb 28th, Saturday [KI-YANG]

Was 'room orderly' today – played 2 games of chess with Fairley and lost 1!!! Beat Dergel in 2 games. Did a bit of reading and started trying to revise 'trigonometry'.

March 1st, Sunday [KI-YANG]

Heard that we have landed troops in France! No parade after all on account of weather. Lazy day. Spent morning working out trig. formulae. Did a bit of reading. Mr Gwok came up again for English lessons. Dull day again.

March 2nd, Monday [KI-YANG]

Usual dull and damp weather. Played a few games of chess and did usual doodling & dreaming.

March 3rd, Tuesday [KI-YANG]

Feeling decidedly 'browned off', probably because I have got a cold. Went to our No. 3 Chinese Coy HQ at 14th Battalion HQ. Saw them training – squad drill – with the exception of a few officers & NCOs the men are very sloppy and decrepit-looking – this appearance is rather exaggerated by their untidy & bulky clothing. Marched back a long way round across the inevitable muddy paddy field paths – it is very tiring to the eyes walking a long distance because one has to be watching one's feet all the time as the paths are narrow & slippery – so that when one looks up everything is dazzling and painful to the eyes. Usual evening.

March 4th, Wednesday [KI-YANG]

Rotten day – raining most of time. Practice for tomorrow's 'demonstration scheme'. Our squad is the 'enemy' and occupy pillbox and guard bridge which are to be demolished, live ammo is to be fired 100 yds. to R. of pillbox, and primes, booby traps, etc. to be fired in our near vicinity. Miserable evening as have a cold.

March 5th, Thursday [KI-YANG]

Went sick this morning as was very feverish with cold last night. Felt a bit better today. Miserable & wet day again. Played chess with Capt. Moffat in afternoon – 3 games – he beat me each time. Spent evening in bed with bad headache.

March 6th, Friday [KI-YANG]

Route march today – following compass bearings from clue to clue – plenty of strenuous hill-climbing but quite enjoyable altogether. Had good hot bath in afternoon. Usual evening. Mr Gwok came in again for instruction in English.

March 7th, Saturday [KI-YANG]

Lazy morning – cleaning rifle, etc. Robbie held a 'General Knowledge' test in afternoon – I got magnificent score of 38%! Was on guard tonight. Had meeting with Mr Lancaster re English lessons, which Anderson & I are to give at High School in town.

March 9th, Monday [KI-YANG]

Miserable day with rain. Went to railway station (about 15 miles from here) by truck – had 'chow' there – spent remainder of day lecturing to Chinese squads (via interpreter) on 'railway sabotage'. Fixed Bickford igniter on rail with orange fuse and det. – railway officials refused to run train over this part of line for fear of damage to line and rolling stock! They diverted trains onto other line – but eventually sent a locomotive preceded by 8 trucks over the line to explode our dets.! Tried a det. on the line – did not explode till last of wheels had passed over it. Usual lazy evening.

March 10th, Tuesday [KI-YANG]

Went on river in sampan – a showery day. Went about a couple of miles up the river and went for a walk from W. bank – got caught up in heavy rainstorm. Haversack rations again – I feel we are missing too many good dinners. Sun came out strongly in afternoon – walked back from pagoda across high hill. Had good bath on return here. In the evening went to the High School just outside Ki-Yang. The class were quite intelligent boys of about 16. Their pronunciation was far better than I had anticipated – but they have little idea of what they are reading – quite an interesting evening. News tonight that all objectives in Rangoon have been demolished – looks like the beginning of the end.

March 11th, Wednesday [KI-YANG]

Very hot and sunny day today. Had compass march lasting all day, culminating in the climbing of a very high and steep hill – then to find to my extreme annoyance that 'Sally' was not at the objective at the top but down in the valley – and all our climbing was just so much waste of energy. Had a good bath on return home – after beating Fairley back (he had said he could get back within an hour – it took me 1 hr. 50 min!) Spent evening working on designs of roadhouse. Heard that Rangoon occupied by Japs.

March 12th, Thursday [KI-YANG]

Spent morning in Robbie's room, tracing map of our op. area – under difficulties of no suitable tracing paper or instruments. Continued same in afternoon. Night scheme – Anderson and I had a cushy part in scheme – we proceeded to the farm at foot of 'One Tree Hill' and awaited arrival of Ely's and Sally's parties there. Sally arrived at about 20.30 – but Ely didn't turn up – so we left for

home at about 23.45. Had a good quiet smoke at farmhouse – farmer brought out a bowl of 'cha' (in reality – hot water) and I sat in lee of a bug-infested haystack, listening to the immense chorus of bullfrogs and thinking of London – long drinks of lager and ginger beer shandies. A very precarious march home across paddy fields.

March 13th, Friday [KI-YANG]

Lazy morning spent in bed after exertions of last night. Ely's party came in at dawn after having slept out all night. Continued mapping in afternoon. Spent evening chatting and playing around at designing houses.

March 14th, Saturday [KI-YANG]

Continued mapping this morning. Heard that we are to march 300 miles in 12 days to our op-area!! If and when we go, we shall have little food and much hardship. Am a bit annoyed with myself now, for being in China, in view of the present state in Burma etc., – for it seems evident that we cannot now achieve our object of drawing troops into China away from Malaya!!! Had committee meeting this evening re 'English teaching'. Spent evening in usual lazy manner.

March 16th, Monday [KI-YANG]

A wet and miserable day. Scheme all day. Took haversack rations – marched to 'buff cottage', did recoy of 'saddle' from there during morning. Wrote up op. orders in afternoon. Carried out attack at 20.00 hrs. after much crawling about in mud and paddy fields. Australians acted as enemy – very difficult to move quietly as it was a still and rather chilly evening, consequently no frogs croaking as covering noise. Got good meal on return to camp – thence to bed.

March 18th, Wednesday [KI-YANG]

A very warm and pleasant day. Went to town in morning in an endeavour to purchase mapping pens, tracing paper etc., – got some red ink, brushes and water colours. Started work on some new maps in CO's room – have to have them finished by Friday evening – very difficult with lack of implements, etc. Read interesting article in Geographical Mag – 'Oil Wells etc'.

March 21st, Saturday [KI-YANG]

Mapping again this morning. Went to see General Han about translation of place-names for maps. More work in afternoon. Spent evening writing to Bel. Heard rumour that we are to receive some mail shortly.

March 22nd, Sunday [KI-YANG]

Spent most of day preparing pack for 2 days' march we are starting tomorrow – what a weight! – not looking forward to this march at all.

March 23rd, Monday [KI-YANG]

Not a march after all – had to stay in and finish maps for CO. Very warm day but didn't see much of it. Usual lazy evening listening to gramophone and reading. Received mail! – airgraph from home and letter dated 3rd January from Bel.

March 24th, Tuesday [KI-YANG – HOSPITAL]

Maps in morning – felt rotten in afternoon so went for a walk – rather feverish about tea time so went sick and was put in 'dock' with temp of 102 – pains in eyes and back – think I've got malaria.

March 25th, Wednesday [KI-YANG – HOSPITAL]

Still feeling pretty rotten with bad headache and backache but temp has gone down a bit. Wally came in to see me.

March 26th, Thursday [KI-YANG – HOSPITAL]

Feeling a bit better. Quite comfortable here. Tea made of Indian tea with milk! 4 Chinese nurses here – very pleasant. Spent day reading. Visit from Robbie.

March 30th, Monday [KI-YANG]

Discharged from hospital this morning. Carried on with maps in afternoon. Very cold and wet today. Spent evening reading. News not very good – Japs still pushing N. in Burma.

April 1st, Wednesday [KI-YANG]

Good scrounge today – went down to riverside with haversack rations – stayed there till about 1400 hrs. sunbathing, swimming, and reading, a very warm and sunny day. Lying there in the warm sun after a swim, I thought myself away to the sunny sands in Devonshire of 3 years ago – felt just a bit homesick and longed for a drink! – there's nothing to drink here but Chinese tea – and hot water! Spent evening as usual reading and doodling. There are some quite good books in the school library now.

April 3rd, Friday [GOOD FRIDAY – KI-YANG]

A surprise this morning – hot cross buns (quite good) for breakfast. Had lecture from CO this morning about being 'browned off' and the necessity of keeping 'face' with Chinese, etc. Went for walk with Wally – to river across country – back along bank to pagoda and thence home.

April 5th, Sunday [KI-YANG]

Went sick this morning with bad eye – got an eyewash. Had service this morning from a Bishop – didn't enjoy it much as it was definitely a C of E service. Rather cold and chilly today.

April 11th, Saturday [KI-YANG]

Scheme with Chinese today – they have little idea of field tactics – they talk too much & too loudly and have no idea of taking cover. There were 2 Chinese dressed up as peasants to act as runners – they made themselves conspicuous by walking about doubled up, etc., instead of acting part as peasants. Have no confidence in these men. Usual evening.

April 12th, Sunday [KI-YANG]

Lazy day today. Spent morning trying to repair camera – of which the shutter won't function properly.

April 14th, Tuesday [KI-YANG]

Told to stop mapping. Everything points to a move in the near future and I think it won't be to our original areas but to Burma or Thailand. Fatigues all day packing stores. Went to 'school' in evening as usual – spoke about railways, etc. Rain all day again with long rumbles of thunder in early mornings.

April 16th, Thursday [KI-YANG]

Rain continues to pour down relentlessly all day – paddy fields are flooded to path level. Fatigues again today. Read 'Patchwork' by Beverly Nichols – pretty mushy!

April 18th, Saturday [KI-YANG]

Were officially told today that we are going back to Burma – good news! – will probably have to march most of it – only 2000-odd miles!! Received some comforts today for squad – tins of fruit, cigarettes, tobacco, etc. Rain again today as usual. Had party tonight with whiskey!

April 21st, Tuesday [KI-YANG]

A lazy day – went to canteen all the morning – got caught by Sally – and a dressing down by Robby! Move seems to be postponed into indefinite future. Watched basketball in afternoon. Our team wins. Started reading 'South Riding' by Winifred Holtby – very good. Mail today! – 1 letter Air Mail from Father – posted 22/12/41. Hot – sunshine again.

April 25th, Saturday [KI-YANG]

Had a wakeful night on account of stomach-ache. No parades today. Final of basketball today – we won. Squad had a 'dinner party' in barrack room, consumed some of comforts – I unfortunately could not participate on account of stomach-ache – no food today. Weather – showery.

Big Flowery Hill

April 27th, Monday [LI-CHIA-PING]

Left school this morning at 09.00 according to schedule, came to stores at about $^1/_2$ mile from Li-Chia-Ping, the railhead. Spent morning loading stores on railway wagon and guarding same – had 'chow' in Chinese restaurant in town – plenty of pretty girls 'for hire' here. Spent night on guard in railway wagon with Elliot. Weather – heavy rain.

April 28th, Tuesday [LI-CHIA-PING]

Fatigues again all morning loading demolition stores on railway wagon. Lunch & dinner in town – chow is quite good. Very amusing in evening on balcony of restaurant awaiting meal – usual crowd gathered to stare up at us – Dergel & Stock 'entertained' crowd by awful singing and a few words of Chinese such as 'hshen-hsai nee-ti chih fam' – they were clapped, hissed and assailed by 'ding how' & many 'poo-how's. A huge crowd had gathered right across the road. Spent night on guard again. Weather – very warm and dry.

May 2nd, Saturday [IN TRAIN]

Left store house in FSMO at 12.00 hrs., marched to station at Li-Chia-Ping. 'Excellent' accommodation in steel goods wagons – 1 wagon per contingent! Eventually made ourselves fairly comfortable by removing boots and spreading out ground-sheets & blankets. Slept sardine fashion. Very stuffy and uncomfortable. Rations – bully and bread. Weather – wet.

May 3rd, Sunday [IN TRAIN]

Train travelled very slowly with many stops. Had a shower at water-
tank last night. Stopped at a station about 100 miles from Li-Chia-
Ping at 08.00 – stayed there till about 13.00 then heard bad news
that we are returning to Li-Chia-Ping – move to Burma cancelled –
no reason apparent yet. News from Burma seems bad – Lashio
and Mandalay having fallen. Train returned towards Li-Chia-Ping.
Weather fine.

May 7th, Thursday [LI-CHIA-PING]

A very pleasant morning from about 05.00 till 08.00 after which it
got very hot. Had a good march up from back of billets to treetops
on high hill on skyline about 6 miles away; had to cross river to get
there. Quite a gentle but long climb thro' some sweet-smelling
woods. There was a monastery on top of the hill and the monk in
charge was a very pleasant Mongolian, rascally-looking fellow with
a merry twinkle in his eyes, he reminded me of Charles Laughton;
they insisted that we should have food, and on account of 'face' we
had to wade thro' some strong garlicked vegetables and some quite
good red-rice; the best dish was a fried chapatty of what seemed to
be grain husks and dried fish – it looked suspiciously like manure.
I took some photos of the priest at which he was very pleased and
requested copy of photographs. Weather – fine in morning, rain
later in day.

May 10th, Sunday [LI-CHIA-PING]

Went for walk up 'Big-Flowery-Hill' again, had some excellent swimming in a very clear pool, visited the monastery again, discovered from interpreter that the chief priest is very surprised that we can't speak Chinese – he thought Captain Annand was a Chinese because he spoke Chinese – very surprised at the fairness of my hair, and my blue eyes. Scenery was glorious. Writing this on top of hill on a flat slab of smooth rock which juts out from the hillside and commands an excellent view. The sun shines down on a long lazy line of silver-edged clouds floating passively in a translucent sky of powdered blue above the hazy blues and purples of the horizon's mountains which are revealed by a break in the line of rugged hills stretching across the valley below. The valley is silvered with the watery patchwork of paddy fields which occasionally burst out in brightest greens, darkened by the trees and farm buildings on hilly arisings. Below the frowning rock on which I sit the hill drops steeply down and divides into two spurs, silken green in the sunlight and hanging in folds like some exquisite and liquefying gown – so smooth are they that I feel as if I could reach out my hand and stroke them. A breeze stirs – and a mischievous fluffy white cloud sails over his lazy silvered fellows and darts behind the hill – brushing against its silken sides with a caress. A very pleasant walk back, then the usual lazy evening – very hot tonight.

May 11th, Monday [LI-CHIA-PING]

Everybody seems convinced that we shall be sent to India, altho'
I am not very optimistic. Japanese seem to have advanced up
Burma Road to Lun-Ling! Big battle in Pacific. Very fed up with
being cooped away here doing nothing constructive or even
destructive. Weather – very hot and sunny.

May 13th, Wednesday [LI-CHIA-PING]

Fatigues this morning erecting tent for CO. Went fishing with
explosives this afternoon, got quite a good catch – several small
'mandarin' fish and two large fish about 3 ft. long – a very good
afternoon swimming after the fish. Usual evening smoking and
chatting – very hot and stuffy. Weather – hot and sunny.

May 14th Thursday [LI-CHIA-PING]

Went up 'Big Flowery Hill' again for the day, had good swim in the
pool and a lazy day of sunbathing. Had a few games of chess in
evening – played chess against Major Moffat in evening, managed
to beat him once, also played three games with Sgt. Leake – but he
was poor resistance. Weather – hot & sweaty again.

May 15th, Friday [LI-CHIA-PING]

Guard again today. Had spot of swimming in little pool at back here.
Started reading 'Gone With The Wind'. Reported sick with 'Hong
Kong feet'. Weather – hot & sticky again.

May 19th, Tuesday [LI-CHIA-PING]

A very pleasant march across the hills today, thro' sweet-smelling pine woods and thickets of bush and wild flowers – well populated with butterflies of many colours. Passed thro' many plantations of bamboo – in many places it was being cut down into thin strips about 5'0" long – these strips are placed in bundles in deep vats made of clay, covered in lime and water and left to rot, thus forming the basis of the paper made hereabouts. Took a few photos from the hilltops. No news yet about our future. Weather – warm, sunny.

May 25th, Monday
[LI-CHIA-PING, AL FRESCO AT TOP OF HILL]

Came up 'Big Flowery Hill ' today – until tomorrow night with Wally, Fairley, Rusty, Nardie and Andy. We brought stores and tents up by coolie – but only one tent complete with set of poles – just rigged up a shelter from the sun which is very hot and penetrating. Had some good lounging and swimming, and a couple of excellent meals. Our supper consisted of a mixture of Scotch broth, mushroom and chicken soups, followed by chicken, then fish rissoles – and a trifle made from cake, tinned fruit and tinned milk. A glorious sunset tonight – starting with a dark copper sky, which changed to gold and blue in a few seconds – took some photos of the sunset. Pleasant sing-song – message from camp in Morse by torch. Weather – very hot, but windy.

May 26th, Tuesday [LI-CHIA-PING]

Had an excellent sleep last night – no mosquitos and a pleasant wind, all accompanied by a huge frog orchestra from the pond by which I slept. A good breakfast this morning – and more swimming. Took photos of Chinese children. Descended from hill at about 5.00, still very hot in the sun.

May 30th, Saturday [LI-CHIA-PING, BIG FLOWERY HILL]

Came up here after demolitions finished this morning – very hot. Have erected tent as shelter from sun. Had usual good swim. Discovered our old water supply dried up – but found another source – equally cold. Very hot here today, but a bit cloudy and windy in the evening. Had quite a good meal here, grilled pork chops and eggs; but our rice pudding made of rice, eggs & sugar wasn't much of a success as the rice had not been soaked for long enough. Had a pleasant smoke of Balkan Sobranie this evening.

23 26.5.42 Big Flowery Hill

24 26.5.42 Big Flowery Hill

Journey By Train, Junk, and Sampan

June 6th, Saturday [HEN-YANG]

Left Li-Chia-Ping railway station at about 13.00 and arrived at the railhead Hen-Yang at dusk. The bridge over the river here has been demolished & the passengers are transferred by ferry. We had a meal by the riverside here and then fatigues all night until about 3.30 Sunday morning loading stores & kit into junks.

June 7th, Sunday [IN JUNK – RIVER HSIN]

Junks started off at about 06.00, two convoys drawn by steam launches, about 12 junks in each convoy. Last night I dumped my kit & myself into a very small waterlogged compartment with Joe Nardie & kit. Awakened this morning in about 6 inches of water & very dirty, uncomfortable & miserable – it had been raining all night. Got ourselves sorted out during the day – rained most of day, very cold and miserable. Had to take cover under hatches several times on account of aircraft. Saw 8 Jap bombers pretty low overhead this morning heading for Hen-Yang; saw 8 again this evening. Tied up by shore for the night.

June 9th, Tuesday [IN SAMPAN – GOING EAST]

Transferred from junk to sampan early this morning and took a branch river going eastward. This is a very pleasant and clean river, not nearly so wide as the other, with green scenery on either side. The sampan is being drawn along by man-power via a long rope from the mast. The crew have just gone on strike and two men have left – the other two now refuse to work; after much arguing and threatening we get one more & carry on. 6 planes passed over this

morning – heading for Hen-Yang. Stopped at about 16.00 after having travelled only about 4 miles. We are travelling against the current which is at times very strong! Nardie and I had job of taking rations up to 'Australians' & 'Malayans' who are about a mile back – had my first effort at handling Chinese craft. Had some good swimming during the day. Weather hot and pleasant – I think this has got 'Broads Cruises' beat.

June 10, Wednesday [IN SAMPAN – GOING EAST]

Up early this morning, had a wash and a swim – but a late start as we were waiting for Chinese soldiers to help with hauling of boats. Planes overhead again this morning and sounds of machine-gun fire and bombs being dropped – from direction of Changsha. Also sound of machine-gun & light-artillery fire from N. of river – Jap front only about 5 miles from here. Late in afternoon came up to a weir constructed across river to drive large water-wheels 20-30 ft. in diameter for irrigation purposes. Weir was in two parts diagonally across the river – constructed of wooden posts – some places difference in water level 2 ft.; crossed first in a gap in the rapids; but all boats got stuck at second weir. We got ashore and hauled boats in by rope as they came up. I climbed on the water-wheel out into the weir to catch ropes as thrown by boatmen then along the muddy slippery bank to haul the boats across and some pulling it was, time & time again we were whipped into the river by the taut rope. Last boat of our contingent came thro' as it was getting dark – first rope snapped – I went out for another – which also snapped – so we left them there till the morning. Meanwhile all the boats had gone some miles up river & most of us were left in the nude! Blondie and I tried a short-cut thro' the woods, and frightened the inhabitants of one village by our nakedness; at the next we provoked mirth – but got a fellow to show us the direction of the river. There we picked up Elliot on a sampan & proceeded to find the rest of the 'convoy' – it was now dark with plenty of sandbanks everywhere, the two crew sullen and unwilling to work – I used up the remains of my energy poling the boat upstream. Good meal on arriving at camp for night. On guard tonight.

June 11, Thursday [IN SAMPAN – GOING EAST]

Started off at about 7.00 after a wash & swim. Feel very sore and painful all over after last night's experience – cuts and scratches all over my feet, legs and posterior from crossing the race against the water-wheel where I was bashed against the bamboo. Crossed another weir very shortly after starting – got across without ropes. Came to another weir about midday, a double one as last night, got right up to first weir by poling but then got caught in current & swept back. All of us went overboard & took rope – walking up on the stony bottom against the terrific current – my feet ached as never before! Then we had to get rope across main stream to an island to get a tow across the weir – the current here was very strong and the water deep – the Chinese soldiers refused to cross – so Nardie crossed with the rope & I swam across to help him hold it. One Chinese soldier crossed but got panicky half way across & shouted for help – we managed to get him out. After much heaving & feet aching we got clear. Crossed another double weir this afternoon but crossed without much trouble. Have hove-to below yet another one. Another very hot and fine day. Took two photos of boats crossing weir.

June 12th, Friday [IN SAMPAN – GOING EAST]

Up early as usual, had swim & shave. Glorious sunset last night – had good meal on river bank – bathed in its lemon yellow glow & listened to the musical organ-like hum of the water wheels. Crossed about 7 weirs today and consequently didn't travel very far, were fairly lucky in crossing, being towed by a junk with a capstan. Stopped near a small town – very clean place with even-paved streets – people better dressed than at Ki-Yang – shops very spacious, clean with polished counters & neat cupboards, etc. Weather – very hot.

June 13th, Saturday [IN SAMPAN – GOING EAST]

Usual early rising & a shave & swim. Had a good swim last night before turning in – it was very sweaty last night. Very hot again today, but bit of a breeze later on. Am now sunburnt to the colour of mahogany – wearing nothing but shorts all day & not always that! Travelled a fairish distance today as weirs more spaced out as we passed thro' a bit of hilly country where irrigation not so necessary. Some beautiful scenery hereabouts – placid river bounded by trees. Banks of river & hills have trenches & gun posts. Living on bully biscuits, etc., supplemented by local food. Abundance of peaches and plums hereabouts – consequently have had much stewed fruit; peaches are not yet ripe & I can't quite understand why they pick them so soon unless it is poverty. Went into village near here in search of food – village has been bombed & burnt-out by Japs during their 5-day occupation of last year. On guard tonight.

27 11.6.42 Between Changsha and Liu-Yang

28 18.6.42 Near Liu-Yang. Demolished railway bridge in background

June 15th, Monday [IN SAMPAN – CHANGSHA-LIU-YANG]

A very tiring day commencing at 04.30 until 18.00, towing all six boats nearly all the day, till my feet are cut in ribbons & my arms aching. Have lost count of number of weirs crossed today. Passed thro' hilly wooded country – many peach and plum orchards. Can see mountains in the distance and they seem very high. Hauled up for night on island in midst of rapids – stormy tonight, has been hot as usual all day.

June 16th, Tuesday [IN SAMPAN – CHANGSHA-LIU-YANG]

Usual early start 04.30 – had a disturbed sleep last night on account of rain. Had a bloody awful morning towing all 6 boats thro' about a mile of very fast-flowing rapids – it took us about 4 hours. Heavy storm broke out about midday when we were in the midst of hills, first flash of lightning ran right down the valley in which we are sailing and just missed a tree about 50 yds. from our boat, this followed by most terrific crack of thunder I have ever heard. Transferred a lot of the stores and ourselves to smaller shallow-draught sampans – 8 to the contingent in order to speed up our movement. Rain all day – river swollen and swift.

29 16.6.42 At rest after crossing rapids

30 17.6.42 My boatman on small sampan

June 17th, Wednesday
[IN SAMPAN – CHANGSHA-LIU-YANG]

Usual early start – but was able to lie in bed this morning as there was only Nardie & myself on this boat. River very swollen & swift – many rapids. Had to do a bit of hauling of the larger craft. Intermittent rain all day. Still travelling thro' very green hilly country towards Nin-Yang. Saw rather a peculiar sight this afternoon – a long thin bamboo pole at water's edge with about a dozen large birds of the 'falcon' type perched on it (presumably tied by their feet) – they were being washed by a small boy throwing water over them – I'm still trying to puzzle out their usage. Another peculiar & fairly common sight here is a large bamboo tub floating down the river propelled by a man with a brush – reminds me of the three men of Golgotha (or was it?). Discovered birds mentioned above were cormorants used for fishing.

June 20, Saturday [IN SAMPAN – NEAR HU-YANG]

Started off for Gwang-Du this morning but only travelled a few miles as river in flood with a very strong current. Had a hellish night last night sleeping on top of baskets of unequal height & resilience, fighting a losing battle against bugs, and any period of inactivity on their part was punctuated by snores from the 'la-ban', grunts from his wife and squeals from the two children, all of whom are bundled into a space about 6 feet long at the bows. The woman is blind but manages to do quite a bit of work in poling the boat, her youngest brat must be about a year old but spends all day at the breast – I'm beginning to have some doubts about this beauty of the female form & motherhood stuff. Weather – dull and hot.

June 21st, Sunday [IN SAMPAN – NEAR HU-YANG]

Stopped here yesterday at midday waiting for river flood to subside – was warm & bright in the evening. Was on guard last night. By 04.00 hrs. this morning river had dropped 5 ft., at that time terrific rainstorm lasting till 08.00, by which hour the river had risen again another 6 ft.; we had rain off and on all day, and by 20.00 hrs. I reckon the river had risen a good 12 ft. and doubled its width. Spent all day here (mostly sleeping) waiting for river to subside. Rations seem to be getting meagre & it is difficult to purchase anything locally.

July 1st, Wednesday [NEAR CHANG-FENG]

After a very restless night. Started off at about 06.00 this morning in terrific rainstorm, had to plunge thro' rushing waters up to our knees, where path had been washed away by floods. Got soaking wet after a few minutes despite my unsoldierly equipment of umbrella. Same trouble again with coolies, had to do a bit of shooting again. *[Ed: This refers to the firing of shots in the air to dissuade coolies from deserting.]* About midday we were held up by flooding river but by 1 o'clock it had dropped by about 3 feet!! Reached school building near Chang-Feng about 15.00 feeling very wet and tired after plunging thro' paddy fields & torrential streams. Had good bath & changed into what dry clothes I have left. My basket had been dropped in water & nearly everything soaked including my precious negatives & developed films. Have billets in schoolroom, just picked up a calendar (issued by British Ministry of Information) with a photo' of Hampton Court – brings back old memories. About 6 miles today.

July 2nd, Thursday [PEI-PU]

Started off at about 07.00 hrs. this morning – very fine morning. Made good progress early in morning following a river upstream most of the time. Trouble with coolies deserting again. Some glorious scenery along the river, but path very narrow and difficult – many parts washed away by flood – evidence that river had flooded to height of 20 ft. above present level. After midday started climbing very steep hills, then followed a stream downstream. Very tired and browned off at end of day, couldn't get fire to burn as no dry firewood. Had very little food today – 4 biscuits. Weather: very hot and sweaty all day. Distance 17 miles.

July 3rd, Friday [TUNG-KU]

Early start at about 5.30 this morning. Followed river downstream all day but path very difficult – washed away by floods in many places and very stony in others. My legs and feet very sore with sweat-rash and blisters. Distance reputed to be 10 miles – but it was the longest 10 miles I ever travelled. Arrived here at about midday, had few showers in morning but cleared up at midday. Stores taken across river but we are staying in hotel here until tomorrow as insufficient room in stores till 'Malayans' move out. Are to be here until 8th, but there seems to be a hell of a row on about a coolie shot by the Aussies. This is a very small one-street place built against very steep and high rock (which provides good Air Raid Shelter). Looks quite picturesque from upriver on account of peculiar rock formations.

July 5th, Sunday [TUNG-KU]

Went shopping for Coy in morning. Went to church at 09.00 – quite a good attendance. Service in tiny Mission Hall decorated with Biblical pictures in Chinese. The missionary has been here 10 years without relief! – gave quite a good service but what I really enjoyed was singing hymns again. Took over accounts, etc., from Anderson. Had a little party in evening to celebrate Andy's promotion, (Shuker also promoted to Cpl.) – had some decent Chinese wine.

July 6th, Monday [TUNG-KU]

Went across river to H.Q. early in morning, crossed bridge about $1/2$ hr. before its collapse – (heavy rainstorm last night). Sorted stores etc., then tried to get boat back across – but could not. Eventually found ferry-boat about 2 miles downstream and tried to bring it up to cross (in order to avoid being swept on to rapids lower down). After about 3 hrs. hard poling, pulling, etc., gave up as bad job. Stayed night at H.Q. Plenty mosquitos. Weather – heavy rain showers all day.

July 7th, Tuesday [TUNG-KU]

Got back across river early this morning (as it had dropped 5 ft. during night). Went back again later with stuff for HQ & to sort stores. Spent most of day on accounts, etc. Weather – rain showers all day.

July 8th, Wednesday [TUNG-KU]

Usual routine. Rumour has it that we move tomorrow morning. Tried to get across to HQ today but river too high. Weather – rainstorm all day.

July 9th, Thursday [TUNG-KU]

Diarrhoea pretty bad today – went across to HQ in morning. Went out in evening, had a spot of wine with Robby – told me that any commission had got as far as Chung-King. Weather – showery. Today's move did not materialise.

July 10th, Friday [TUNG-KU]

Once again rumour 'hathn't it' – i.e. no move today. Squad played Chinese at basketball – suffered their 1st loss. Spent most of day on accounts, routine work, etc. Weather – fine.

July 11th, Saturday [TUNG-KU]

Nothing doing again today – looks as if we shall be stuck here for some time. Everybody 'browned-off'. Started reading good book 'Farewell Romance' by Gilbert Frankau. Weather – very hot & stuffy – had good wash in river.

July 12th, Sunday [TUNG-KU]

Cook today (very busy day fitting in other work with cooking). Very hot and stuffy all day. Scenery here delightful in sunshine.

July 13th, Monday [TUNG-KU]

Heard today that we move tomorrow. Busy day on accounts, etc. Nardie, Marshall, Geen & Fairley not coming on with us when we move. Fairley going to India! Got caught in terrific rain shower today – soaked thro' – very annoying as I shall have to pack wet kit tomorrow. One of Malaya Contg. died today – typhoid.

July 14th, Tuesday [TUNG-KU]

Move cancelled again. Feeling rotten today – diarrhoea and general listlessness. Weather – showery.

July 15th, Wednesday [TUNG-KU]

No move again today. Very warm and depressing. Stomach still bad and my thoughts are ever turning to food – the glorious meals that Mother made, and even army meals outside China – the mere mention of feeding in a book once again stirs the imagination. Must snap out of this lethargic state. Weather – hot.

July 16th, Thursday [TUNG-KU]

Cook today. Busy day on accounts & cooking, diarrhoea bad again. Tried to dry out photographic negs which got damp on journey up but fear a good 50% are ruined. Weather hot & warm. One of Aussies died – typhoid. Due to move tomorrow.

July 17th, Friday [TUNG-KU]

Move did not materialise. Felt pretty rotten with diarrhoea. Went for walk in afternoon with Rusling to high hill on horizon – didn't quite make it but walked some 12 miles in very hilly country. Some excellent scenery. Weather – hot.

July 18th, Saturday [TUNG-KU]

Felt rotten again today – very hot & stuffy again. Played 'deck tennis' in afternoon then had usual wash & swim down with current in the river. Rumour again has it that we move tomorrow.

July 19th, Sunday [SAN-TU]

Moved out at 13.00 hrs. today to accompaniment of fire-crackers. Only 5 miles march to here – but was dead beat & with temperature when we got here. Stomach still bad. Only about $1/3$ of our original strength moved up here. Marshall, Nardie – left behind for treatment. Shuker, Geen, Stock in hospital so total strength with interpreter is 8. Weather – very hot & stuffy. Distance – 5 miles.

July 20th, Monday [T'A-T'UAN]

Left San-Tu at 4.30 this morning, reveille 3.00. Marched 50 mins to the hour and arrived here at about 9.30. Fortunately we were in the shade most of the time for after 07.00 the sun was very strong. Some glorious scenery, small irregular pimply hills & valleys winding willy-nilly thro' paddy & sword-grass. Followed river most of way – most magnificent gorge scenery, but difficult to appreciate under marching conditions. Had good cold shower from well water on arrival here. Weather – very hot & sunny. Distance 13 miles.

July 21st, Tuesday [T'A-T'UAN]

Stayed here again all day – as Caldwell has temp of 105 F and MO must stay with him. Very pleasant here if one could get good food and water. Stomach still bad. Had swim in river during afternoon. Weather – very hot & sultry.

July 22nd, Wednesday [T'A-T'UAN]

Started off at 05.00 after 3.00 reveille – felt very rotten at 1st halt & was sent back by CO – very annoying because I think I could have 'made it' OK. There are about 6 of us left here with MO hope we move on very soon. Weather – hot.

July 23rd, Thursday [T'A-T'UAN]

Felt OK first thing in morning – then about midday got a terrific attack 'amidships' which brought me out into a cold sweat & put the whole of my body in a tight cramp. Doc gave me a shot of dope and after while spasm passed off – but belching continued all day. Apparently attack caused by a lack of 'calcium' in system – have consumed 18 calcium pills today – 90 grm; and am on strict diet of poached eggs, glucose etc. Feel very weak. Weather – hot & thundery.

Aug 2nd, Sunday [T'A-T'UAN]

Usual day – which means getting up at about 07.00, having a wash & shave in the cold well water. Breakfast – usually poached eggs. Then a lazy morning sleeping or reading rather disturbed by sweat & flies. Lunch usually bully and rice pudding, afternoon spent as morning. Evening meal always consists of 2 chickens either boiled into a stew or roasted + veg – marrow & beans – followed by stewed pears or one of MacDonald's famous cakes. The evening is best part of day here, we sit on the doorstep after a nice cold wash, and have a chat until about 20.00 when we retire to our hard and uncomfortable beds. Am feeling much better now, but still my waking and dreaming hours are filled with thoughts & visions of good food; yesterday I started to read Eric Linklater's 'Poet's Pub' again because it has many tasty mentions of food – have suffered from this obsession for several weeks now. Food is getting a bit scarce here now, we had difficulty in obtaining our 2 daily chickens today, sugar of course is very expensive & rarely to be obtained; we were lucky enough to get a catty of arrowroot today. Peaches here are very small & hard & usually maggoty – sometimes we manage to get good-sized pears – but I have not yet found a ripe one, and they are still hard after a couple of hours stewing. The weather today has as usual been very hot – bright sunshine from 07.00 until 18.00 hours, glorious sunset. Took a few photos today, but camera not in very good condition, damp seems to get into films, and mildew has got on inside of one of lenses – also on shutter which also is slightly out of action.

Aug 3rd, Monday [T'A-T'UAN]

Bit of unusual news today, 13 planes flew over at high altitude at SE direction – can't imagine where they were making for, assuming them to be either Jap or American. Col. McDougall passed thro' at about midday. Letter from Col. Miller says that I am to report back to Ki-Yang, so now I don't feel so fed up about going back.

Aug 4th, Tuesday [TUNG-KU]

Started off at 05.00 this morning with Hollingsworth + 6 coolies & 2 chairs. Walked all way to San-Tu, 13 miles, and then took chair for couple of hours – quite comfortable but rather degrading to be carried by one's fellow man. Very slow journey. Arrived here about 16.00 hrs. Saw Col. Miller – he doesn't know anything definite about my future. Hope I shall soon be able to push off from here. Weather – very hot.

Aug 6th, Thursday [CHANG-FENG]

Left Tung-Ku at 05.00 hrs. after usual haranguing with coolies… Reached P'ei-Pu at about 11.00 (10 miles)… After P'ei-Pu started climbing high range of hills which divide Kiangsi and Hunan provinces, once again saw large waterfalls on opposite mountain-side, altho' this time there was little water flowing. Arrived here 16.30 after nearly 12 hrs. on the road – very hot & we were in the sun most of the time. Consumed large quantities of cha. Travelled about 20 miles in all…

Aug 9th, Sunday [KWANG-TU]

Spent morning examining S.T. grenades and cleaning out loose explosive from cases. Found two grenades less than $1/2$ full & very leaky, exploded these along with loose liquid from boxes – caused much excitement among locals. Weather – hot with short storm & raining in afternoon.

Aug 14th, Friday [KWANG-TU]

Remainder of stores arrived today – spent busy morning repacking 'bully' into baskets. Had 'special' meal this evening, Heinz baked beans, poached egg, & broken biscuit pudding & coffee! – very enjoyable. Finished reading 'Hell On Ice' – very good story of terrific endurance. Rain all day – hills blotted out in a grey mist of rain & heavy lowering clouds overhead all day – distinct drop in temperature – scenery completely changed & like a raw day on the N. Devon Coasts. Insect life very active in evenings.

Aug 17th, Monday [LIU-YANG]

Left Kuan-tu at 07.10 hrs., arrived Ku-Kuan 30 li away at 10.15 hours. Arrived here at 15.45 hrs. having travelled 70 li, my coolie was very fast & took few halts. Found this hotel 'Chin-Chin Lu Kuan' O.K. – quite a smart place for this part of China; have large room & clean-looking bed – good service. Visited magistrate about boat – have to wait until Wednesday – hope it doesn't drag out any longer than that. The weak 'blue' ink is annoying so have refilled with this smudgy ink – very difficult to get good ink in China. My 'boy' here is very attentive – took me to magistrate to arrange boat, prepared bath, etc. – I think he considers himself very superior to other 'boys' as he has a 'few' words of English – 'yes', 'A,B,C,D',

'us' – which he seems to use for 'I' – 'tea', and 'jam' pronounced 'gem'. This room has a stone floor and is very cool and airy. Had quite good meal, marrow soup, fried eggs, rice and some good sweet wine. After dinner had visit from magistrate and my 'boatman' for Wednesday + a crowd of the usual gaping satellites, after much talking and difficulty explaining in my best Chinese, elicited following news – sail on Wednesday, $25 without food, $40 with food. The boatman is a very 'piratical'-looking gent. (Received $400 from Captain Gunn.)

Aug 19th, Wednesday [LIU-YANG]

Decided 'tummy' ache this morning, too much Chinese cooking I suspect. By 15.00 felt decidedly ill. Boat departure had been postponed until 16.00 hrs. Decided to phone Gunn that I had malaria and get some quinine sent on. Went to telephone at far end of town – spent 1 hr. trying to get thro' and make Chinese understand that although Gunn wasn't on phone they could send a messenger for him. Efforts interrupted by sudden inburst of excited Chinese saying 'English men come' – so naturally I went back to hotel – nobody had arrived – they simply wanted to tell me that the boat was ready – I told them to go to hell – and myself went back to 'phone – no results. Eventually went to another 'phone about 4 miles away and got thro'. Gunn said Col. McDougall was coming thro' in a few days and would bring up quinine. Arrived back at hotel in state of collapse to find my room being used as a brothel! – was I mad! No sleep. Felt as if my head was covered with suitcases, at other times imagined myself locked up in a small drawer. Had nothing to eat.

Aug 20th, Thursday [LIU-YANG]

Very bad again – no food – day seemed to be ages long and myself a mere egg-shell! Chinese soldiers arrived in afternoon with quinine and tin of milk. A real good fever at night.

Aug 23rd, Sunday [ON RIVER TO CHANG-SHA]

Left Liu-Yang 07.00 in very small boat + 2 chin-yan-pings, 2 boat crew + woman and 2 kids, also a load of peas – the peas were excellent. Made good progress. Weather – very hot and space restricted. Covered about 70 li today.

Aug 24th, Monday [ON RIVER TO CHANG-SHA]

Started off at 05.00 hrs. and didn't stop until 21.00 hrs. La-ban then started off-loading his peas much to our annoyance trying to sleep. Must have travelled 100 li or so.

Aug 25th, Tuesday [CHANG-SHA]

Arrived here about midday – at Human Bible Institute, a very 'posh' place with hot & cold and every 'mod' con! Found Robbie still here, sick with a fever of some sort. Had excellent meals – bread, milk etc!

Aug 26th, Wednesday [CHANG-SHA]

Still feel very shaky today but hope to move off to Chung-King as soon as Robbie is fit. Went out around town in afternoon, bought pair of shoes, $140. Weather: pleasantly cool.

Aug 27th, Thursday [CHANG-SHA]

Usual lazy day with good grub. Spent morning pumping water. Went to town in afternoon, bought suitcase, $50. Moving to Hen-Yang tomorrow morning. Cool today.

Aug 28th, Friday [HEN-YANG]

Left Changsha at 07.00 hrs. this morning; 3 hrs. ferry journey to railhead, had to wait till 15.00 for train to depart. Arrived here, missionary place about 20.00 hrs. and so to bed. Weather: hot.

Aug 29th, Saturday [IN TRAIN – HEN-YANG TO KWEILIN]

Left Hen-Yang by train 18.00 hrs. – 1st class sleeper. Robbie left us with no money – had trouble about sleepers as we couldn't afford to pay for same. Had good night's sleep. Weather – hot & sticky.

Sept 2nd, Wednesday [PARIS HOTEL – KWEILIN]

Felt pretty groggy today. Spent all day working on 'framed structures'. No lunch today as stomach bad. 7-course dinner again tonight – met some R.A.F. fellows who are working on airfield here – also an American woman who has escaped from Hong Kong. Went to 'flics, saw 'Confessions of Nazi Spy' – sound effects bad – made worse by chattering and nut-crunching of audience. Back to restaurant afterwards and consumed two bottles of wine.

Sept 3rd, Thursday [PARIS HOTEL – KWEILIN]

3rd year of war today! Air-raid at 06.30 this morning lasted till about 12.00 hrs., all shops etc. shut and everybody except us evacuated town. Had no breakfast until it was all over. Spent morning working on stress calculations. Went to flics in evening, saw 'Lady Hamilton' – very good – better cinema than other – better sound effects. Very hot all day. Stomach bad.

Sept 4th, Friday [PARIS HOTEL – KWEILIN]

Stomach still bad today. Another air-raid warning this morning – didn't last long – breakfast as usual. Visited Capt. Eardley, has decided to send us by road owing to plane difficulties. Leave on Sunday morning 07.00, arrive railhead same day 22.00 hrs. (express train). Wired Hemmingway for transport to meet us at railhead. Drew another $500. Spent most of day working out stress calculations. Met the American woman from Hong Kong in restaurant – she bought us lots of wine – it appears she was a brothel mistress in Hong Kong so therefore has stacks of money – told us of atrocities in Hong Kong & her life story – quite an interesting evening. Got back at about 02.00 hrs.

Sept 5th, Saturday [PARIS HOTEL – KWEILIN]

Had breakfast with American woman. Went to Eardley for cash etc., – had to wait hell of a time. Drew $2000 from him; got ticket 2nd class – train leaves 07.00 hrs. tomorrow. Stomach still pretty bad. Met American woman again at dinner time – but made excuses and came back early. Packed kit, paid hotel bill – 300 dollars! Very expensive for so scruffy a place – but I suppose we had to pay for the rent of the rats as well.

Sept 6th, Sunday
[IN TRAIN – KWEILIN TO CHIN-CHENG-CHIANG]

Went to station in truck – picked up Robbie's suitcase. Air-raid at 07.00 – train pulled out into siding – stayed there till all clear at 11.00. Met Mr & Mrs Chow – Chinese Canadians from Hong Kong and a Miss Chow – who are to travel to Ching-Ling with us. Stayed up till about 23.00 talking to Miss Chow who speaks very good English – and seems to be "a gay young thing".

Sept 7th, Monday [CHIN-CHENG-CHIANG]

Train arrived here about 02.30, continued sleeping until about 05.30 then went out and located Railway Guest House where we are staying. Our rooms had been booked OK – one room with 4 beds! Eventually got other rooms during day. Maggie and I have a double room for $24 – quite clean and comfortable. Chinese chow - not at all bad! Met couple of fellows – Golden – (a naturalised Russian from Hong Kong) and Morris from some ambulance unit – who are also waiting for our truck, we all 7 of us feed together, quite a party. No telegram from Hemmingway. Spent most of day gossiping.

Sept 10th, Thursday [GWAY-YANG]

Left hotel at about 05.00 hrs., finally got started at 06.00 hrs. – hell of a crush in the truck. Driver tried to get an army major on as well – but I wasn't having any. Stopped for lunch at about 10.30 then carried right on till we reached here at about 20.30, considerable rain during afternoon – and altogether a very uncomfortable journey. Hemmingway a bit peeved about bringing all these "yellow fish" thro' – but very kindly allowed Miss Chow to stay the night.

Sept 11th, Friday [GWAY-YANG]

Late arising had breakfast at about 10.00 hrs. – fried eggs, toast, butter and jam. Miss Chow left with Hemmingway, who is going to try and fix her up – eventually got her a temporary job. Maggie and I had a look around the town in the afternoon – prices are terrific. Telegram from home 7/9/42 – arrived Chung-King 9/9/42 – they have received my April letters (received July). We are to proceed to Kumming & report to Consul General as soon as possible – looks as if we will go straight to India from there. Have had enjoyable meals all day, but tonight's dinner I think caps the lot – nothing elaborate – steak, potatoes, greens & tomatoes, followed by pancakes & jam – but the cooking!! – nearest to home cooking I have yet experienced in China.

Sept 14th, Monday [GWAY-YANG TO KUMMING]

Left Gway-Yang this morning on charcoal-driven truck at about 11.00. Huge gang of illicit passengers on board most of day – driver collected various sums up to $100 from them – must be making good money. About midday three tough youths hopped on back of truck – when we stopped in a town they hopped off and started to beat up the driver – I suppose he must have collected their money one day & then dumped them. Arrived this place at dusk, boarding house not too bug-ridden. Very hungry, sunk 4 bowls rice + etc. Only travelled about 80 miles today.

Sept 19th, Saturday [KUMMING]

Got on truck en route for Kumming at about 10.00 hrs. with two F.A.U.s, one a Col. McClure, a Canadian doctor who speaks excellent Chinese & is real good company. Hell of a squeeze on the truck, which was carrying petrol drums full of wine – to be converted into motor spirit; very dusty, and we got absolutely filthy. Puncture about 50 kilos out which meant an hour's delay. Truck only went to within 19 kilos of Kumming – got a bus there – Tried to charge us 80 dollars for our luggage but McClure talked the bus driver out of it by making him lose face. About 2 kilos on, bus was attacked by gang of soldiers, throwing stones etc., – dragged driver out & started to beat him up under supervision of an officer! – McClure once again saved situation – we all tumbled out of bus & presented a solid & bulky front to protect driver – McClure told soldiers that they had behaved very badly in front of foreigners etc., and we went on our way. On arrival here went to Y.M.C.A, dumped our kit and had our first shower for many days & we needed it! After this refreshing bath went out for Chinese meal – very good. Then phoned consulate, but they didn't seem to know much about us, but said to call round before 09.30 tomorrow. Met a Mr Smith who said he would put us up for night – he has a lovely house. Hot & cold, etc. etc. Travelled about 100 miles today – pretty hot most of time.

Sept 22nd, Tuesday [KUMMING]

Usual long sleep and lazy day. Went into town in afternoon with
Mr Urquart to have our photos taken for passport purposes. Met
Chapman & Gilmoor who arrived here on Sunday with Capt. Wolf –
had some coffee and cakes, bill = $76!!! Over a £1 for what would
cost at home about 1s/6d. Learnt that we are not leaving by plane
tomorrow but are moving to No. 1 Hostel.

Sept 23rd, Wednesday [KUMMING]

Moved into No. 1. Hostel – very chilly reception – apparently British
troops are not appreciated here. Tried to find Chapman & Gilmoor
but apparently they have left. Major Tregear + 2 officers & a sgt.
from Chung-King came round in afternoon, said we are to leave
tomorrow morning. Good grub here.

Sept 26th, Saturday
[CALCUTTA – BRITISH MILITARY HOSPITAL]

Plane left Kumming at about 09.30, a very bright and sunny day.
Very comfortable seat in about centre of plane – Douglas aircraft.
Climbed pretty rapidly and felt it a bit in the ears, apart from that
had a thoroughly comfortable journey – although many people
were very sick as we passed thro' several storm areas with air-
pockets. Didn't get much of the chessboard pattern impression
of the ground below as we were in and above the clouds most of
the time and it was as if we were lumbering thro' colossal snow
fields. On arrival here we were told to wait at Customs for truck
to take us to B.A.S. – unfortunately an ambulance arrived and
took us to hospital, where I have been admitted with septic heel.
Grub very bad.

POSTSCRIPT

John Hay's diary entry for July 22nd, 'Sent back by CO – very annoying,' marks the end of his journey into China. Other written accounts tell us that the 204 Mission staggered on with 'not one pair of serviceable boots between them', arriving at their forward base, Ch'iu-Chia-Kai, on July 26th. Of the 46 men in the Burma contingent who left Kiyang for the forward base, 72% had been stricken by malaria, 40% had suffered from severe diarrhoea or dysentery, and 13% had contracted venereal diseases. Despite the decimating disease and lack of supplies, food, ammunition, and medicines, for weeks the generals at the British Headquarters in Chung-King insisted there would be no withdrawal of the 204. It would seem that this policy was based on reports to the generals of victories achieved by the Chinese Surprise and Penetrating Troops. The purported victories proved to be pure fantasy. Reconnaissance patrols of the area around Ch'iu-Chia-Kai and Nan-Chang revealed a reality of very different dimensions: a firmly entrenched, well-equipped army of 17,000 occupying Japanese troops, commanding complete control of air space. With only 5 officers and 14 soldiers of the Burma contingent fit for active service, and the two other contingents of the 204 equally reduced in number, the men radio propagandist Tokyo Rose referred to as 'Churchill's Butchers' could do little more than watch the Japanese troops from the mountains. The decision to withdraw was finally made on September 14th, and the 204 flew out for India from Kumming, China on October 29th, 1942.